I0786437

Animal Communities
- Revisited -

A clever collection of creature collectives,
And a fun way to learn their group names

By Ari Levitt, MD

Table of Contents

From scientists like Darwin,
    to docs like Dr. Seuss,
        come comments on the nature of community,
for it seems we're not creatures inclined to be recluse
        but need gather together in unity.

For company, or affection,
        or as oft's our predilection
            to seek safety or protection from a threat,
or, to take the opposite view,
        to form a "pack", or "hunting crew",
            since a pack can be a predator's best asset.

But whether running in packs,
        or like insomniacs,
            gathering at night to convene,
all critters meet together,
        in whatever kind of weather
            be they airborne, terrestrial, or marine.
Be they tall, fat, or thin,
        bearing paw, hoof, or fin,
            built as small as an amoeba or a mouse,
it's a fact 'o phylogeny,
        that for the sake of progeny
            all animals at some point must spouse.

'Cuz when more than one loon, raccoon, or baboon
        meets up with it's friends out in nature,
it's a fact that the pair (or however many there)
        have their very own group nomenclature.

Yes it's true,
        more than two
                or three critters in view
                        aren't breaking any assembly laws,
        when as a group or collective
                they gather irrespective
                        of their reason, the season, or cause.

'n if you don't know what to say
        to that group or menagerie
                of beasties you happen to meet,
or what to call 'em properly
        as a host or emcee
                out loud or in manners discrete —

Know we've given our friends of fin, fur, or feather
        who run, jump, walk, crawl, fly, or churn,
specific group names when they gather together,
        which from reading this book you can learn!

Yes, you'll find here in bold,
        for all to behold
                and written unambiguously,
all kinds of critter
        for you to consider,
                and what then their group names might be.

So sit back 'n relax,
      learn a few trivial facts
            to augment your vocabulary.
    Share this book with your friends,
      it's a kind of zoom lens
            for a price that is practically free!

So in case you should ask why it's called a large '**bask**'
      when it's croc's you should chance to encounter,
and not a *flock,* or a *flaggle,* a *boudoir,* or *bedraggle,*
      or a word of more strange or odd banter.

Or while gazing at birds,
    if your at loss for words
        what to call them in manners more terse,
    rest assured, here in bold,
      and for all to behold,
        it's all written
          with wit
            …. and in verse!

— A CADRE OF ANIMAL COLLECTIVES —
PART I: Shorter Verses

In ancient days, beavers raised
>their **families** in dwellings quite crammed,

'til one old care giver
>made 'em move to the river

>>where they said, "So much room — I'll be dammed!"

When buzzards take breaks they do so in "**wakes**",
>— **wakes** are the company they're keeping.

No matter the weather, they're a "**wake**" when together.
>They're even a **wake** when they're sleeping!

A large **pace** of asses, for want of molasses
>told their boss that the **drove** would resign.

Said the boss to the asses, "you don't eat molasses,
>so don't be so asinine!"

When flies swarm in **hatches**, **businesses**, or **clouds**
>they're oft heard long before they are spotted.

You can hear them because when flies flap their flaps buzz
>— which ends if they ever get swatted.

When you send all your piggies to shop at the market
        they'll go there together as a **sty**,
but if sold overseas and you have to transport 'em,
        that's the day that you'll see piggies fly!

Penguins in **colonies** waddle about
        on the Antarctic snow where they're mired,
and each Sunday at three they attend a high tea
        where they always come formally attired.

Together in a **flutter**, butterflies will clutter
        in the air to elude your inspection,
but if and when you see 'em on the walls of a museum
        it's not a **flutter**, but a butterfly **collection**!

The mischievous raven is foremost a maven
        of pranks and of sophomoric schtick,
'n like a **murder** of crows, his delinquency grows
        skipping school by 'cawing' in sick.

When elephants gather to signal each other
        with trumpeting that shatters the peace,
in **herds** they'll convene, the one exception being
        young Dumbo who hangs out with geese.

Crocodiles rest in **basks** when they nest
       together in rooms where their eggs sit,
where, in case of disaster, they know it's much faster
       to put all their **basks** in one exit.

Coots form a **covert** or **cover** in groups
       when together they're shopping for booties.
And when they play tag, all the girl coots in drag
       give all the cute boy coots the cooties.

Though flamingo's form **stands** when they gather in bands
       I'm not sure if this name is that fitting,
'cuz they're not only **stands** when they're standing on land,
       they're also called **stands** when they're sitting!

You've probably heard how sheep, cows, and goats
       will gather in groups far and near.
To avoid all the shouting when they have sore throats
       — they **herd** thus to much better hear!

Two **<u>armies</u>** of frogs met deep in the bogs
       to play baseball 'n count RBI's,
'n though their batting technique
       seemed to me pretty week,
          they were all above par catching flies!

If you see some hippopotami (or a hippopotamus)
        as you travel down a river on a boat,
you may say "while to us one's a hippopotamus,
        two together are more of a **bloat**"

As I sat down to eat some onions and liver
        A **quiver** of cobras slithered by.
Even more than eating liver,
        cobra **quivers** makes me shiver,
                I'm sure you can understand why!

Though a **pod's** a small **herd** or **school** of whales
        (that's a fact that you cannot rebuke),
I once thought I saw a whale swim by
        but it turned out to be just a 'fluke'…

Boris the Tortoise was a very shy tortoise,
        you would never in a **creep** hear him yell,
'till one day with a "bong!" he burst out in song,
        and finally came out of his shell!

While woodpeckers work at whittling wood
        with their peckers in a pecker **descent,**
how much wood could a woodpecker peck
        if the woodpecker's pecker got bent?

In **caravans**, camels,
  those large desert mammals,
    will gather to drink coffee brew,
where the question to ask as
  you serve each a glass, is
    "Do you prefer one lump or two?

Outside his den, the little red fox
  stays alert to the day's fox-hunt sounds,
'cuz he knows that the wolf still runs with the **pack**
  and so too, by gosh, do the hounds!

You might think a large **gulp** of cormorants
  in a **flight** would be hard to follow,
'cuz flying in a **flight** sounds to me about right
  but flying in a **gulp**'s hard to swallow!

Groups of wombats will meet in a **wisdom**
  'cause a **wisdom**'s where wombat's accrue.
Said one wise old fowl, "They're on par with the owl,
  'cause owls in **wisdoms** meet too!"

A **fever** of stingrays swimming at sea
  may gather together at night.
Say some staunch believers, in regards to ray **fevers**,
  "their sting is much worse than their bite!"

When tw**o** or more hawks take flight in a **boil**
      you say that "a **boil** just flew past"
but for ten or more birds, you use different words,
      saying they're flying in a **kettle** or **cast.**

While sipping their soup
      a kitty cat group
           tried to brain-storm a name for their **cluster,**
but between sips of chowder,
      a "**cluster**" or "**clowder**",
           were the only two names they could muster

When a **prickle** of porcupines lays down to rest
      in a nest of their own pick and choosing,
the pricks from the **prickle**
      are worse than a tickle
           — they leave welts and occasional bruising!

Animal sociologists use sophisticated words
      to define complex groupings or cultures,
except when describing the poor vulture birds
      who apparently just hang out with vultures….

Did you hear what the papa buffalo said
      waving to his little calf, Tyson?
Right there in the midst of his **herd**, **troup**, or **gang,**
      he smiled and then simply said "Bison!"

Said a **cast** of crabs to a **bed** of clams,
        "Not only do clams look quite elfish,
when we asked one a favor
        to share it's fine flavor,
            it said "no!",
                How come you're so shellfish?"

Oh where have you been my own turtle dove,
        is your **dole** in a duel briefly met?
to battle foul foes, like a **murder** of crows,
        a **murder** most "fowl", you bet!

Oh where have you gone my true turtle dove,
        is your delinquent dove **dole** taking pause?
To do mischief, I suppose, or like a murder of crows
        passing time with crank telephone caws?

Though a **company** of parrots (called a **pandemonium**)
        is characterized by loud noisome squawking,
most parrots wouldn't agree
        what you hear's cacophony,
            'cuz to them it's just all normal talking.

An "**unkindness** of ravens", a "**conspiracy** of crows"
        are names that you've likely not heard'a,
'cuz what kills me the most is when folks just assume
        that crows only meet in a **"murder"**

If you think that "a **raft** of otters" is silly
        when it comes to group names, just relax,
it's what otters all get
        for getting all wet
                then floating around on their backs.

While bacteria in **cultures** or **colonies** grow,
        — both the good kind and also the villain,
the distinction won't matter if you accidentally splatter
        either one with a little penicillin.

A **hover** of trout might flitter about
        in streams 'neath where people are boating.
It's a healthy **hover** sign to see 'em 'neath the brine,
        — less so if they're ever found floating.

Caterpillars in trees
        will march as **armies**
                'till they transform into butterflies
where in **flutters, kaleidoscopes, rainbows,** or **rabbles,**
        together they'll take to the skies.

When one cockroach scurries, it does so alone,
        but in groups they're an **intrusion** (not a harem).
A cockroach **intrusion** may disperse in confusion
        if you suddenly turn lights on and scare 'em.

While swans group in **banks**, in **teams**, or in **bevy's**,
     peacocks rarely gather in two's.
When they do, on occasion, they're a **pride** or **ostentation,**
     which usually takes place around zoo's

Mares eat oats in **studs** or **flocks**
     while doe's eat oats in **leashes,**
but though little lambs eat ivy in **flocks,**
     they prefer crème brûlée with fresh peaches…

Two porpoises together are never alone
     you may hear them chit-chatter aloud.
'n though two is a company in human terms,
     to a porpoise it's always a **crowd.**

Would you ever believe the word **"crash"** was appointed
     to describe a group of rhinoceros?
No matter they're anointed with schnoz's pin-pointed
     The idea is simply prepos'erous!

Giraffes "crane" their necks in **herds**, **groups**, or **corps**,
     they crane when they're straining to see.
But cranes, though they gather in a **herd** or a **siege,**
     won't their own necks "giraffe" willingly.

While larks in **ascensions** or **exaltations** are met
eagles in **convocations** convene,
and while geese on a pond are called **gaggles** or **plumps**
when in flight they're a **covert** or **skein**.

A **colony** of gulls or a **band** of jays
can be seen flying together or flittering,
but where did those poor little magpies go wrong
for their group to be called just a **twittering**?

The viper is known for it's venomous spit
which can leave you in bouts of delirium.
Should one ask you to lunch with it's **knot, den,** or **pit**,
don't bring wine, just a tourniquet and serium…

When primates play music, it's primarily in **bands**,
wearing hats as their only apparel.
But when they drive home, they do so in fact
as a **cartload** of monks (not a barrel).

A **loveliness** of ladybugs is such a perfect term
to describe the lovely ladies that they are.
They're lovely night and day,
dressed in red 'n black, not grey.
(— though some think the dots go too far)

At dawn or at dusk you might glimpse a **husk**
        of jackrabbits lazily loping,
like corn on the cob, in a **husk** rabbits mob,
        just like antelopes **herd** anteloping…

While hyenas in **cackles** may heckle comic jackals
        sounding much like bad plumbing with a wheeze,
the thing that gets 'em rolling in hysterics on the flooring
        is a joke about cuttin' the cheese.

Great Apes, because they're oft imbued
        with wits to match their crudeness
when gathered together en-masse to brood,
        do so in a **shrewdness.**

The eagle, you've heard, is our national bird
        (a symbol that stands for our nation)
but together when they stand beak-to-beak or hand-in-hand,
        you call them an eagle **convocation!**

If you want to paint a feather, the more paint the better
        to get all the colors just right.
But if you make a deal to paint a zebra **zeal**,
        then you really just need black and white.

Though an **army** of caterpillars strips bear a tree
        on their mission to eat and devour,
their campaigns and forays may take several days
        'cause they move just a few feet each hour.

The home of John Thistle was clean as a whistle
        'til one day he ordered, by phone,
some puppies & kittens, and piglets with mittens,
        which literally thrice **litter**'d his home.

Hedgehogs romp within **arrays**
        'neath rays of sunny weather,
and ferrets are in **fesyns** met
        when they're forming a **business** together.

A restful slumber you will gain
        by nodding off to sleep,
counting in **hirsels**, **packs**, or **droves**,
        those **trips** & **flocks** of sheep!

Parrots in **companies** primarily pair
        to their parrot of perennial choosing,
while oysters produce pearls from their oyster **beds**
        where they love to bed down for some snoozing!

Geese group in **gaggles**, hens hunt in **broods**,
       and ducks fly in **teams** or in **braces**,
'n rats when they race run in **rabbles** down roads,
       … though they rarely wear shoes with pink laces.

Together in **herds** the buffalo roam
       and the deer and the antelope play,
but after the playing should they run through your home,
       I suggest you get out of the way!

In deepest darkest Africa
       where **troops** of monkeys sleep,
a **leap** of leopards lies in wait
       to make it's morning leap

While gorillas gather or group in a **band**
       and in **packs** wolf pups practice their pants,
the largest of mammals to roam o'er the land
       are, you've heard? — **herds** of huge elephants!

Owls convene in an owl **parliament**
       like subjects of British Empirees.
A **clutter** is chiefly for kitty cats meant.
       A **hive** is a commune for bees.…

If you were a **team** of ox-cart oxen
        comprised of an oxen or two,
no matter how strong
        you pulled it along.
                the yoke would still be on you.

In **gangs** or in **rafters** turkeys will meet
        to gobble a treat or share laughter,
but after Thanksgiving, those no longer living,
        join the **gang** in the **rafter** "Here-After"

A **pace** of mules with knobby knees
        ran a race where they almost placed first,
'till they were out-squeezed by a large **swarm** of bees
        who in **hives** live, but fly in an **erst.**

While bathing in the ocean, enjoying that ocean motion,
        should you meet a large jellyfish **"smack"**
stay calm as a statue, they're not going to catch you,
        they just float there, they rarely attack…

When an **ambush** of tigers met a **streak** of tigers
        streaking pellmell through the door,
each could tell that the others
        were, in fact, tiger brothers
                by the colorful streaks that they wore.

Piglets are born in **litters**,
    which are loud (nothing quiet or shy),
'n though pigs-in-a-blanket may make a nice lunch
    more than two in a pen make a **sty**

A skunk, when annoyed, is a thing to avoid
    best to move far away from it's path,
so should you, on the street,
    meet an angry **surfeit**,
        I suggest you don't stir up their wrath,
or what happens next
    will require no pretext
        and will likely result in a bath.

Mr. Fox, that 'ol dickens, will stalk **flocks** of chickens
    when in **skulks** or in **clouds** while it's shady.
then bring to his den a rooster or hen
    for the gal there he calls "foxy lady"

When buffalo roam on the range near your home
    they do so in a **gang** or a **troop,**
But when they're in town and lay their chips down,
    I suggest that you bring a large scoop.

Have you ever seen an antelope
        trying to eat a cantaloupe
                in a **herd** while dressed in a sweater?
While you might one day hope
        to see that antelope,
                seeing two ants eloping is better….

Though seagull bird-blokes rarely get jokes
        and their laugh is the silliest I've heard,
the talk on the rock where the seagulls all **flock** is
        there's not a more 'gull'-ible bird.

The designer Ru-Paul made some hippos a shawl
        with matching pink shoes and a blouse.
Cried one hip in the **herd** "Take it off, it's absurd!,
        What am I, a hippo or mouse?"

A single honey badger, with big 'ol badger feet,
        got tired of always standing so he took himself a seat.
A **cete** of badger buddies saw him sitting on that chair,
        with agony of da'feet, and his feet up in the air!

Though the terms used for ants may be different in France
        still they **colonize** regardless of name.
So whether in your pants, or your '*pantalon*' (in France)
        the dance you'll prance is gonna be the same…

When sharks out at sea
      get together for tea
         they'll meet in a **school** or a **shiver**,
Except the hammerhead
      who at home in his bed
         prefers his tea Uber-delivered

At the chicken ball game, one little cluck
      snapped another little cluck with a towel.
While some thought the ref
      should have thrown the **peep** out,
         all agreed that the deed was most fowl.

When gathered in pairs, in dens or in lairs
      all lions meet together in "**prides**",
and establish a tree
      of hierarchy,
         with the male being the one lionized.

Schnauzers are
      a breed of dog
         who never quite learned how to clench,
just so, for this reason,
      whenever you sees 'em,
         the group is described as a **stench!**

A **gaze** of raccoons gazed up at the moon
      in a **gaze** they all gazed there as one.
The gaze the **gaze** gazed at the haze of moon rays
      was gazed due to absence of sun.

Have you heard the good news
      'bout the zoo's two new gnu's?
         It's an **implausibility**
that the gurus of news
      knew the zoo's new gnu news,
         before the gnu's new about me!

Wrens when they warble, do so in **chimes**
      'cuz as far as most people can tell,
they're hard to recognize
      (due in part to their size),
         but somehow their voice rings a bell…

Did I ever mention
    the word is **"ascension"**
        when you talk about groups of skylarks?
— used mostly when you see 'em
    outside of a museum
        or gathered together in parks....

I should prob'ly also mention
    the word is still **"ascension"**
        when talking 'bout skylarks in flight?

No matter or depending
    if they're asc- or desc- ending
        they're an **ascension** regardless of height

Now while skylarks convene in **ascensions,**
woodpeckers meet in **descents,**
    to me it's absurd, but I suppose to a bird
    it might make a little more sense

———————

A **labour** of moles was known to dig holes
    from below and too from above.
The holes were so tight, to maneuver them might
    be akin to donning a glove.
But the moles didn't mind, for holes of that kind
    were to them simply **labours** of love.

Though rabbits together are met in a **bury**,
    a **colony**, a **warren**, or **nest**,
if you place a lone bunny on top of your tummy,
    it's like putting a hare on your chest!

A group of bunny rabbits
    is also called a "**fluffle**"
        due much to their habits
            of flopping when they shuffle.
In the event of a kerfuffle,
    stuff the **fluffle** in a duffel,
      — it'll muffle the kerfuffle,
        and avoid all further truffle!

A **group** of young pigs is a **drift**, **drove** or **litter**.
    or if older, you call them "**swine**" - OR -
… it's a **team** or a **passel**, if they're hogs (it's that facile)
    but enough with the pigs — they're a boar!

    [Except in the case of Sammy….]

Sammy the boar, a devout herbivore,
said he wouldn't eat beef, pork, or flounder,
    which sounded insane
      whenever he'd explain
        his reasons to the boars of his **sounder**.
Though the **sounder** of swine simply couldn't divine
    why he'd dine on a fare so effete,
      he'd, in turn, never hassle the hogs of his **passel**
        by admonishing their choice to eat meat.

There once was a bear, with a large derriere,
        and a penchant for drinking vermouth,
            who refused to e'er share that liquor so fare
        with the other bears of his bear **sleuth.**
'Til in a turnabout his liver gave out
        due directly to things of such ilk
as drinking all that booze,
        which he tended to abuse,
            'til his doc switched him over to milk.

While a prairie dog community
        is called a **colony**,
            one which lives underneath the earth's furrow,
coterie's the word
        for describing, you're heard,
            those who live in just one single burrow
— which also applies
        to a small enough size
            or "**unit**" of your own fellow man
since a "**coterie**" of humans, strangely enough
        defines an exclusive **clan**

Congregations of crocodiles will gather together,
in a **nest**, a **bask**, or a **float**.
And while the name of the latter
makes sense for the fatter
crocs that are shaped like a boat,
and the fact that for fun,
they'll **bask** in the sun,
basking in **bask**s neath those rays
leaves no room to ask
why we call them a **bask**,
it's just what the word basking says!
Still what gives me no rest is
why they're called **nests**,
it's a name they must truly regret,
since it's much more akin
to something avian,
like a penguin, a duck, or egret.
"So, why nests?" I asked
to a small silent **bask**
of crocs I ran into one day,
but came no reply
as I stared eye to eye
awaiting to hear what they'd say.
'Til a wizened old heron
who noticed my staring
pulled me aside to explain,
why, though they seem fierce,
crocs never pierce
the silence with sound or refrain.

He said, "Regardless of whether they've something to say
          'bout whatever might've gotten their goat,
                    any croc on a lawn,
                         you've seen there mid-yawn
                              usually has a frog stuck in it's throat…"
It wasn't the question I'd set out to find
          an answer to, but with a grin,
                    the croc winked its eye,
                         and affirmed with a sigh
                              the truth of that information.

———————

A solitary panda is rare to behold,
          especially one dressed up in britches,
which sometime they'll do if the britches are blue,
          and their shorts are in need of some stitches.
Though it helps to explain the strange but apt name
          that for small groups of pandas are meant,
                    since eating bamboo with a blue-wearing crew
                         is for them an **embarrassment**.

———————

A brilliant young bass was top in his class
          but he had even loftier goals:
to earn his PhD in ichthyology
          (that's the study of fish and their roles)
When he finally did pass, his class asked en masse,
          *"Should we call the young bass Dr. **Shoals**?"*

A **bevy** of quail
      tried to take sail
            on a breeze fairly high in the air,
but missing their tail
      their **drift** was a fail,
            and they landed not too far from there.
But a friend from the **covey**
      met them all lovey-dovey
            and bid them good cheer, *savoir faire*

———————

Swans when they fly
      up high in the sky
            fly in a **wedge** formation.
But out on the pond
      it's a **ballet** of swans
            that makes such a great **lamentation**.
And swans at the levy
      are a **bank** or a **bevy**
            according to one wise old drake,
though he still prefers a "**ballet** of swans"
      — 'cuz it reminds him so much of "Swan Lake"

For long days and night
      a **brood** of termites
            made a **nest** for it's **colony** and **swarm,**
establishing a station
      in the very foundation
            of the house that I use to keep warm.
Not to be rude, but my house isn't food!
      and this isn't a frat or dorm,
so for them to digest my house, as a guest,
      seems to me to be pretty bad form…

———————

A **dule** of doves, a **flight** of doves, and a **dole** of doves of
note,
      all met together,
            in inclimate weather,
                  inside a little dove cote.
Said the **dule** of doves to the **dole** of doves
      "looks like we'll be here all night"
            Came no response from the **flight** of doves,
                  'cuz by then they had taken their flight.

Barracudas out at sea
      swim in a **battery,**
           whenever they're not swimming alone.
But a **bat'ry**, by and large,
     describes a thing that holds a charge,
        (like the one used to power your phone).
Which makes this next tale
      somewhat hard to assail
         … but still well-deserved of a groan:

A **battery** of bar'cuda, riding three to a scoota'
      pulled up at a club called "The Barge",
When the bouncer saw the three,
     he let them in gratuitously
      — that's admission without 'dditional charge.

but why would the Barge
     not want a charge
        from a **battery** it lets in for free?
If it were me and the 'cuda,
     I could'a, would'a, should'a
        at least charged for 'lectricity!

———

An **array** of eels met a **rookery** of seals,
      whose pups were so young they were teething.
Said the **array** to the **rookery**,
    by hook or by crookery,
      together we eels form a **seething**,
Said the **rookery** back, "Now listen , Jack,
    we're a **rookery,** a **trip**, or a **herd**,
      whether swimming or sleeping,
        it's the company we're keeping,
          that defines us by that sort of word…

When hunting season comes around
    and hunters get ready to fire,
they might, to the bogs, bring a **mute** of hound dogs,
    for tracking their prey through the mire.
Though it's strange the word **mute** is used to impute
    the hound — mute means "quiet"; "non-violent"
so when folks here start sayin',
    "there's a **mute** out there bayin'
      that mute is, for me, nothing silent!

Some dolphins in their **school**
　　　were studying 'bout the rule
　　　　　and uses of 'habeas corpus'
to prev<u>e</u>nt false impr<u>i</u>sonment,
　　　if shown a perp's true intent
　　　　　were accid<u>e</u>ntal (ie., not done on *porpoise*).

Now the thing that's so cool
　　　is the dolphin's large **school**
　　　　　was acclaimed an "a-cl<u>a</u>mmed-ed" univ<u>e</u>rsity
by a panel of clams,
　　　and some large coral fans
　　　　　who lauded the **pod's** diversity —
for bravely letting in
　　　a minority blue fin
　　　　　to a majority of dolphin-finned courses,
along wth a scallop
　　　and a horse who couldn't gallop
　　　　　(which holds true for most any sea horses)

They also let in,
　　　without complaint or chagrin
　　　　　a cross-dressing tranny clown fish,
and a pair of hip hake,
　　　who were heard, when they spake,
　　　　　to use words like "fabu" and "delish".

A lobster, a turtle, and a horseshoe crab
　　　(all known to be quite hard-shell plated),
despite their unique
　　　defensive physique,
　　　　　were also matriculated.

… Which just re-affirms
        there exists, without terms
                or trimesters (that's 'terms' numbering three)
  in oceans and pools,
        some very special schools
                for creatures who live in the sea!

———————

In Boston, near Philly, a stallion and filly
        were once overheard to say
"As far as **herd**'s go, we'd make a fine show!"
        (followed up by a whinny and neigh)
"If we sired a **team**, or a **rag**, or a **pair**
        of colts, we'd have no remorse"
but the **herd** never heard what the stallion observed,
        'cuz by this time the horse had gone hoarse.

———————

Bullfrogs will gather with others to "croak"
        in "**armies**", though I can't say just why.
The word "croak" can invoke both a sound that is spoke,
        but can also mean "croak" as in "die"
So when folk hear it spoke that a frog up and croaked
        it remains then a challenge to discern
                if the croak was a croak said aloud as a joke
                        or it involved its being placed in an urn.

In the calm of the day
	if I see a squirrel **dray**
		(otherwise known as a **scurry**),
flittering about,
	up & down, in & out;
		racing around in a hurry —
I'll watch each one's acts
	but just can't relax
		'cuz their fray gives me great cause to worry.

———————

A silent group of tadpoles
	never spoke aloud
not while underwater
	swimming in their **cloud**,
It wasn't that they feared to wake
	a predator bringing death,
		It was simply that they couldn't talk
			and also hold their breath

———————

Though I new that it would cost a lot
	to see a group of ocelot
		reciting snarky sonnets in the park,
since all they knew how
	to say was "meow"
		— I'd not heard a more catty remark

— HUMANS —

Humans have the most diverse words I know
    to describe their own groups, yes it's true.
There are more than I fear I could possibly list here.
    but lets start by recounting a few:

a collective, a company, a band, a class,
    a cartel, an organization,
a posse, a faction, a troop, an attraction,
    a circle, a clique, congregation,

a club, a society, a party, a crowd,
    a gathering, a bevy, or bunch,
a league, an assembly, a plenary, a gang,
    or a simple get-together for lunch,

a cadre, a syndicate, a people, a nation,
    a meeting or melding of sorts,
a tribe, a relation, a crew, a formation,
    a collection of friends or cohorts,

a conglomerate, a convocation, an army, or association
    an ensemble, assembly, or throng,
a crib or a cluster, a huddle, a muster,
    a meet-up, a folk sing-along,

a scout troop, a pack, a union, a coven,
    a clambake, a sit-in, or scene
are just a few terms that help us describe
    what we call it when people convene.

—— **SUMMARY** ——

As you have now read
        if you've followed the thread
                of terms herein listed for you,
there's quite a collection of choice (or selection)
        for naming the creatures we view,
                — who gather in groups
                        like baboons do in **troops**,
                or like **packs** made of Sheepdogs or Scots,
                like kittens in **litters** (the cutest of critters),
        or like snakes who just curl up in **knots.**

'n if you're trying to explain
        the term or group name
                to address them in just such an instance,
I hope that your reading this book truly has
        provided you no small assistance.

And might even inspire,
        an inkling of desire,
                — like our section on human professions {*see below*} —
to take a little stab
        at your very own vocab
                or to offer a few new suggestions.

'Cuz, like we define
        how creatures combine;
                how they collect and/or gather in lots,
perhaps there's a name you can lend to your brain
        to describe your own "gathering" of thoughts… :

When you're thoughts come together,
        what would you call 'em?
                Use your imagination!
Pick any word;
        you can choose one you've heard;
                or come up with your own new creation!

For example, my own thoughts I often describe
as a **"coven"** of confabulation;
        a **"hatch"** of ideas,
                a **"meeting"** of mind,
                        a **"speckle"** of speculation.
I might even say a **"skulk"** of ideas
        (**skulk**'s the term that we used for the fox).
The point is to have some fun with the words,
        and if you can, think outside of the box:

Invent something new,
        and then when you do,
                tell a friend.
                        …. heck, tell everyone!
And if your endeavor
        proves something quite clever,
                I'll know that my work here is done….

So, in sum, thanks for reading
        'bout animals meeting
            'n for stretching your mind 'round the bend.
Now there's little left to do, except say to you,
        "Best of luck!"
            … and also:

— The End —

== SOME NEW SUGGESTIONS ==
For Human Groupings
by Profession

== HUMAN GROUPINGS BY PROFESSION ==

*Although the following terms are completely made up,
wouldn't they be fun to have as the official descriptors for each
of the respective human professions they are parodying?*

"a **concentration** of frozen orange juice packers"
"a **bunch** of grape farmers"
"a **lot** of real estate agents"
"a **hoard** or cheapskates"
"a **load** of dishwashers"
"a **combination** of lock-smiths"
"a **batch** of beer-makers"
"a **great deal** of poker players"
"a **fleet** of really fast runners"
"an **assortment** of florists"
"a **cluster** of star-gazers"
"a **battery** of Duracell bunnies"
"an **inventory** of inventors"
"a **caste** of plaster manufacturers"
"an **order** of waiters or cooks"
"a **range** of mountain climbers"
"a **range** of stove manufacturers"
"a **league** of deep sea divers"
"a **knot** of rope-makers"

"a **ring** of circus performers"

"a **denomination** of people who recuse themselves
	from being nominated"

"an **arrangement** of interior decorators"

"a **rearrangement** of even better interior decorators"

"a **form** of IRS employees"

"a **type** of transcriptionists"

"a **quintessence** of people who smell five different
	odors at once"

"a **score** of test-takers"

"a **suite** of candy-makers"

"a **roundup** of shepherds"

"a **patchwork** of quilters"

"a **conjunction** of english majors"

"a **reservoir** of french reservation makers"

"a **preponderance** of people who ponder, just before
	they begin pondering"

"a **gaggle** of people who gag on bagels"

"a **number** of statisticians"

"a **clutch** of hand-shakers"

"a **troop** of heavy or noisy walkers"

"a **denomination** of coin collectors"

"a **quarter** of coin collectors"

"an **acquisition** of museum curators"

"a **number** of mathematicians"

"a **set** of volleyball players"

"a **collection** of fund-raisers"

"a **compilation** of record producers"

"a **flight** of pilots"

"a **slew** of gladiators"
"a **heap** of leaf-rakers"
"a **stack** of librarians"
"a **stockpile** of warehouse employees"
"a **ream** of paper manufacturers"
"a **cache** of money handlers"
"a **heckle** of comedians"
"a **sampling** of wine-sellers"
"a **company** of CEO's"
"a **congregation** of rabbi's"
"a **bulk** of body builders"
"a **union** of marriage counselors"
"a **registry** of cashiers"
"a **convocation** of con-artists who have made
    conning their vocation"
"a **selection** of sommeliers"
"an **ovation** of musicians"
"a **cumulation** of weathermen/cloud watchers"
"a **precipitation** of meteorologists/weather reporters"
"a **lode** of coal miners"
"a **schmear** of bagel makers"
"a **joining** of plumbers"
"a **fabrication** of manufacturers"
"a **piecing together** of puzzle makers"
"a **medley** of musicians"
"a **club** of golfers"
"an **outfit** of clothing-makers"
"a **remnant** of seamstresses"
"a **party** of politicians"

"a **potpourri** of aroma therapists"

"a **mishmash** of hummus-makers"

"a **mixture** or soup-makers"

"a **batch** of cupcake-makers"

"a **shift** of seismologists"

"a **parcel** of postmen"

"an **ante** of your mother's sisters"

"a **collection** of toll-booth operators"

"a **bevy** of people serving beverages"

"a **bale** of hay pickers"

"a **bale** of people who collect twine"

"a **bale** of bail bondsmen"

"a **hearing** of judges, or court appointed attorneys"

"a **hearing** of audiologists"

"a **conspiracy** of lawyers"

"a **clutch** of manual transmission makers"

"a **circle** of geometry teachers"

"a **Bounty** of paper-towel users"

"a **conflagration** of pyro-technicians"

"a **burst** of fire-works vendors"

"a **fusion** of welders"

"a **boom** of sailboat mast manufacturers"

"an **attraction** of shipping magnets"

"an **axis** of gyroscope makers"

"a **barrage** of bomb manufacturers"

"a **genus** of brilliant thinkers"

"a **sprinkling** of cake decorators"

"an **alignment** of auto body repairmen"

"a **treasury** of coin collectors"

"a **ring** of telephone operators"

"a **ring** of jewelers"

"a **ring** of bathtub cleaners"

"a **consolidation** of corporate merger specialists"

"a **smidgen** of people who've ever attempted to cross-breed a smelt with a pigeon"

"a **file** of office secretaries"

"an **encompassment** of navigators"

"an **integration** of calculous instructors"

"an **incarnation** of boutonnière designers who specialize in carnations"

"a **symbol** of percussion players"

"an **organization** of organ players"

"a **séance** of people who say 'aunts' using the British '*änts*' pronunciation (vs, the American '*ants*' pronunciation)"

"a **miscellany** of mistletoe farmers"

"a **concourse** of airport employees"

"a **volume** of novelists"

"a **smack** of corporal punishment supporters"

"a **swarm** of entomologists"

"a **muster** of mustard makers"

"a **flock** (or nest) of ornithologists"

"**thousands** of kilometer measurers"

"a **bank** of money-lenders"

"a **bank** of people sitting by the river"

"a **syndicate** of newspaper reporters"

"a **fraction** of statisticians"

"a **sleeper-cell** of napping prisoners"

"a **branch** of horticulturists"
"a **multiplicity** of calculator manufacturers"
"a **lion's share** of cat breeders"
"a **convention** of conventional people"
"an **intersection** of traffic guards"
"a **convening** of convenience store clerks
"a **concavity**" of Spanish speakers with cavities
"a **prominence** of people who stick out"
"an **abundance** of people who dance with their hair
    in a bun"
"a **correlation** of people who, at their core, believe
    they can relate to everything"
"a **manifestation** of people who post manifestos in
    train stations"
"a **citadel** of people who prefer to sit when they listen
    to Adele"

=== GLOSSARY ===

======== **GLOSSARY** ========

*The following terms are referenced in the poem
(listed here in alphabetical order):*

above par: better than normal

admonish: to warn or reprimand someone firmly

amoeba: a single-celled animal that catches food and moves
about by extending fingerlike projections of protoplasm

asinine: extremely stupid or foolish

asset: a useful or valuable thing

augment: to make something bigger, better, or greater by adding
to it

avian: relating to birds

banter: casual conversation

bask: to lie or sit enjoying the warmth of the sun

baying: the sound made by a hound or dog

booties: little baby shoes

boudoir: french for "bedroom"

braying: the sound made by a donkey

British Empirees: poetic license for "people of the British
Empire"

cacophony: a loud and unattractive noise

cadre: a small group of specially trained people

chagrin: distress or embarrassment at having failed

commune: a group of families or single people who live and
work together sharing possessions and responsibilities

comprised: to consist of; be made up of

convene: to meet together

cooties: a child's term for an imaginary germ or disease that one
can catch by touching a person who is disliked or
socially avoided

cordage: cords or ropes, especially in a ship's rigging

crème brûlée: a dessert of custard topped with caramelized
        sugar
croc's: (poetic license) short for crocodiles
cross-dressed: wearing clothing typical of the opposite sex
delinquency: neglect of one's duty.
delinquent: someone who neglects their duty
delirium: an acutely disturbed state of mind that occurs in fever,
        intoxication, and other disorders and is characterized by
        restlessness, illusions, and incoherence of thought and
        speech
'delish': poetic license for 'delicious'
derriere: French for one's bottom or backside
discern: to recognize or distinguish between
discrete: in a quiet or unassuming way that doesn't call attention
        to yourself
divine: [verb] to guess, to foretell, to anticipate, to prophesize
duffel: short for "duffel bag" — a large canvass bag
Dumbo: the flying elephant of Walt Disney cartoon fame
effete: decadent and self-indulgent
emcee: the person acting as the master of ceremonies at a party
endeavor: to try
Empirees: (poetic license) someone who belongs to an
        'empire'
en-masse: al together, as one
e'er: poetic license for 'ever'
'fabu': poetic license for 'fabulous'
facile: easy
filly: a female horse
flittering: moving about in an erratic way
furrow: a ridge of dirt or earth
gullible: easily tricked, someone who believes anything they're
        told
'habeas corpus': a law that states that a person cannot be kept in
        prison unless they have first been brought before a court
        of law, which decides whether it is legal for them to be
        kept in prison
hake: a kind of fish

heckle: to harass a stand-up comedian during a performance
harem: a group of female animals sharing a single mate
herbivore: a plant-eating animal
here-after: from here on
hierarchy: an arrangement or classification of things according
        to their relative importance
hip: slang for 'cool', 'popular', 'in vogue'
hoarse: a person's voice sounding rough and harsh, typically as
        the result of a sore throat or of shouting
imbued: to inspire or permeate with a feeling or quality
impute: to imply or suggest
ichthyology: the study of fish
inclimate: severe or harsh weather
ilk: a group of items of the same type
insomniac: someone who can't sleep at night
invoke: to appeal to or call on (a deity or spirit) in prayer, as a
        witness, or for inspiration.
irrespective: regardless of
kerfuffle: a commotion or fuss
lauded: to be praised
lionize: to treat as a celebrity
loping: running or moving with a long bounding stride
marine: pertaining to the sea, ocean, or water
matriculated: to be enrolled at a college or university
maven: an expert or connoisseur
menagerie: a group of animals
manifesto: a public declaration of policy and aims, especially
        one issued before an election by a political party or
        candidate
mire: a stretch of swampy or boggy ground
mired: to become stuck in mud
mischievous: showing a fondness for causing trouble in a
        playful way.
mistletoe: a plant associated with Christmas
molasses: a sweet, thick, dark, syrupy substance made by
        boiling the juice of the sugar cane plant

"murder most fowl": a spoof on "murder most foul", from
           Shakespeare's Hamlet (I.v.27-28)

muster: to collect or assemble

nigh: just about, near

nomenclature: a name for something

oft: (poetic license) short for 'often'

pandemonium: loud, noisy chaos

par: means average; "above par" is better than average

pecker: slang for a bird's beak

pellmell: in a confused, rushed, or disorderly manner

penchant: is a tendency toward something

penicillin: an antibiotic

perennial: lasting or existing for a long time

perp: short for perpetrator, or someone who commits a crime or
          an untoward act

phylogeny: the evolutionary history of a kind of organism

physique: the form, size, and development of a person's body.

predator: someone who hunts or preys on something else

predilection: a preference or special liking for something

prepos'erous: poetic license for 'preposterous', or unbelievable

pretext: an ostensible reason or excuse

progeny: one's children or offspring

RBI: in baseball, short for "run batted in"

rebuke: an expression of sharp disapproval or criticism

recluse: favoring a solitary life

recuse: excuse oneself from a case because of a possible
          conflict of interest or lack of impartiality

refrain: to stop oneself from doing something

remorse: a feeling of deep regret or guilt

resign: voluntarily leave a job or other position

'savoir faire': (French) tact, knowing how to handle a situation

schnoz: slang for 'nose'

schtick: (Yiddish) a person's special talent, interest, or area of
          activity

serium: poetic license for 'serum'

sired: gave birth to

smelt: a kind of fish

sociologist: a person who studies human groups and behaviors
sommelier: a person who serves wine
'spake': poetic license for 'spoke'
spouse: [verb] to get married, take a mate
terrestrial: pertaining to the land
terse: short
tranny: slang for 'transexual'
truffle: poetic license for 'trouble'
ornithologist: someone who studies birds
Uber-delivered: food delivered by an Uber driver
unambiguously: clear and without question or doubt
urn: a tall, rounded vase with a base, and often a stem, especially one used for storing the ashes of a cremated person
venomous: poisonous
vermouth: a red or white wine flavored with aromatic herbs
vocation: career
wrath: anger or ire
yoke: a wooden crosspiece that is fastened over the necks of two animals and attached to the plow or cart that they are to pull

ANNOTATED: ANIMAL GROUP NAMES:

These are common (or popularly used) names for describing
animal groups or collectives by their species

ANTELOPES
A HERD of antelopes.

ANTS
A COLONY of ants.
An ARMY of ants.
A STATE or SWARM of ants.

APES
A SHREWDNESS of apes

ASSES
A HERD or PACE of asses
A DROVE of asses.

BABOONS
A TROOP of baboons
A FLANGE of baboons
A CONGRESS of baboons.

BACTERIA
A COLONY of bacteria.
A CULTURE of bacteria.
*Micribiologists call groups of bacteria COLONIES.
A CULTURE would consist of many colonies.

BADGERS
A CETE of badgers

BARRACUDAS
A BATTERY of barracudas.

BASS
A SHOAL of bass.

BATS
A COLONY of bats.
A CLOUD of bats.

BEARS
A SLOTH or SLEUTH of bears

BEAVERS
A COLONY of beavers.
A FAMILY of beavers.

BEES
A GRIST, HIVE, SWARM, DRIFT or BIKE of bees
A CLUSTER, ERST or NEST of bees.

BIRDS
A FLOCK, FLIGHT, or PARCEL of birds.
A POD of birds (small flock)
A VOLARY of birds (in an aviary)
A BRACE a pair of game-birds or waterfowl
A DISSIMULATION of birds.

BISON
A HERD of bison.

BITTERNS
A SEDGE of bitterns.

BOAR (WILD)
A SOUNDER or SINGULAR of wild boar

BOBOLINKS
A CHAIN of bobolinks (whatever they might be!!)

BUCK
A BRACE or CLASH of bucks.

BUDGERIGARS
A CHATTER of budgerigars.

BUFFALO
A HERD, TROUP, GANG or OBSTINACY of buffalo

BULLOCKS
A DROVE of bullocks.

BUTTERFLIES
A SWARM or RABBLE of butterflies.
A KALEIDOSCOPE of butterflies.
A FLUTTER of butterflies.
A RAINBOW of butterflies.

BUZZARDS
A WAKE of buzzards.

CAMELS
A CARAVAN, FLOCK or TRAIN of camels.

CARIBOU
A HERD of caribou.

CATERPILLARS
An ARMY of caterpillars.

CATS
A CLOWDER of cats.
A POUNCE of cats.
A KINDLE, LITTER or INTRIGUE (for kittens)
A CLUTTER of cats.
A COMFORT of cats.
A CHOWDER of cats.Amy Black
A COLONY of cats (usually wild cats)

CATTLE
A HERD, DROVE or DRIFT of cattle.
A MOB of cattle (US and Australia)

CHEETAHS
A COALITION of cheetahs

CHICKEN
A BROOD, CLUTCH, FLOCK, RUN or PEEP of chicken

CHICKS
A CLUTCH OR CHATTERING of chicks.

CHOUGHS
A CHATTERING of choughs.

CLAMS
A BED of clams

COATI (COATIMUNDI)
A BAND of coati (coatimundi)

COBRAS
A QUIVER of cobras

COCKROACHES
An INTRUSION of cockroaches.

COLTS
A RAG of colts.

COOTS
A COVERT or COVER of coots.

CORMORANTS
A GULP (SOLITUDE) or FLIGHT of cormorants.

COWS
A HERD of cows
A KINE* of cows (12 cows are a FLINK)

COYOTE
A PACK of coyotes
A TRAIN of coyotes
A BAND of
coyotes
A ROUT of coyotes

CRABS
A BUSHEL of crabs
A CAST of crabs

CRANES
A HERD, SEIGE or SEDGE of cranes

CROCODILES
A CONGREGATION or NEST
A BASK or FLOAT of crocodiles.
A STRIKER (unconfirmed)

CROWS
A HOVER, MUSTER, or PARCEL of crows.
A MURDER of crows
A HORDE of crows.
A PARLIAMENT of crows.

CUBS
A LITTER of cubs

CURLEW
A HERD of curlew

CURS
A COWARDICE of curs.

DEER
ROE DEER
A HERD, LEASH or MOB of deer
A BEVY of roe deer.

DOGFISH
A TROOP of dogfish

DOGS
A PACK (wild dogs) or KENNEL of dogs
A COWARDICE of curs.
A LITTER of puppies.

DOLPHINS
A SCHOOL of dolphins.
A POD of dolphins.

DONKEYS
A HERD or PACE of donkeys/asses

DOTTEREL
A TRIP of dotterel.

DOVES
A FLIGHT, DULE or DOLE of doves.
A PITYING of turtle doves.
A PLAGUE of doves

DUCKS
A RAFT, PADDLING or BUNCH of ducks on water.
A TEAM, BRACE, BED, FLIGHT or FLOCK of wild ducks in flight.
A BADLING of ducks.

DUNLINS
A FLING of dunlins

EAGLES
A CONVOCATION of eagles.
A CONGREGATION of eagles.

EELS
An ARRAY of eels.
A SEETHING of eels.

ELEPHANTS
A HERD or PARADE of elephants
A CRASH of elephants.

ELK
A HERD of elk.
A GANG of elk (US)

EMUS
A MOB of emus.

FERRETS
A BUSINESS of ferrets.
A BUSYNESS of ferrets.

FINCHES
A CHARM of finches

FISH
A SHOAL, DRAFT, NEST, SCHOOL of fish.
A RUN of fish in motion.

FLAMINGOES
A STAND of flamingoes.
A FLAMBOYANCE of flamingoes.

FLIES
A CLOUD, HATCH, BUSINESS* or SWARM of flies.

FOX
A SKULK of foxes
A CLOUD, TROOP, or COMPANY of foxes.
A LEASH or EARTH of foxes.

FROGS
An ARMY or COLONY of frogs.
A KNOT of frogs.

GEESE
A GAGGLE or FLOCK of geese.
A SKEIN, TEAM or WEDGE of geese (in the air)
A PLUMP of geese (on water)

GERBILS
A HORDE of gerbils.

GIRAFFES
A CORPS, TROOP, HERD of giraffes.
A TOWER of giraffes.
A KINDERGARTEN of giraffes.
A JOURNEY of giraffes.
A KALEIDOSCOPE of giraffes

GNATS
A CLOUD OR HORDE of gnats.

GNUS
An IMPLAUSIBILITY of gnus.

GOATS
A FLOCK, HERD or TRIBE of goats
A TRIP of goats

GOLDFINCHES
A CHARM of goldfinches.

GOLDFISH
A TROUBLING of goldfish.

GORILLAS
A BAND of gorillas
A WHOOP of gorillas.

GRASSHOPPERS
A CLOUD of grasshoppers.

GREYHOUNDS
A LEASH of greyhounds.

GROUSE
A PACK or COVEY of grouse

GUILLEMOTS
A BAZAAR of guillemots.

GUINEA FOWL
A CONFUSION of guinea fowl.
A RASP of guinea fowl.

GUINEA PIGS
A GROUP of guinea pigs

GULLS
A COLONY of gulls.

HAMSTERS
A HORDE of hamsters.

HARES
A HUSK, DOWN or MUTE of hares.
A TRACE of hares.

HAWKS
A CAST, KETTLE (flying in large numbers) or BOIL (two or more) of hawks.

HEDGEHOGS
An ARRAY of hedgehogs.

HENS
A BROOD of hens.

HERONS
A SCATTERING, SEIGE or SEDGE of herons.

HERRING
An ARMY of herring.

HIPPOPOTAMI
A BLOAT of hippopotami (or hippopotamuses)
A RAFT of hippopotami

HOATZIN
A DONGLE of hoatzin.

HOGS
A DRIFT or PARCEL of hogs.

HORNETS
A NEST of hornets.

HORSES
A STUD or STRING of horses (Breeding)
A TEAM, HARRAS, PAIR or RAG of horses (i.e. colts.)
A FIELD, HERD, REMUDA, SET or STABLE of horses.

HOUNDS
A PACK, KENNEL, MUTE or CRY of hounds
Possibly LEASH of hounds (but cannot confirm this fact)

HUMMINGBIRDS
A CHARM of hummingbirds

HYENAS
A CACKLE of hyenas.

INSECTS
A SWARM of insects

JACKRABBITS
A HUSK of jackrabbits.

JAYS
A PARTY or SCOLD of jays.

JELLYFISH
A BROOD, SMUCK or SMACK of jellyfish.

KANGAROOS
A MOB or TROOP of kangaroos

KITTENS
A KENDLE, KINDLE or LITTER of kittens.

LADYBIRDS LADYBUGS
LADYBEETLES
A LOVELINESS of ladybirds.

LAPWINGS
A DESERT or DECEIT of lapwings.

LARKS
A BEVY of larks.
An EXALTATION of larks.
An ASCENSION of larks.

LEMURS
A TROOP of lemurs.

LEOPARDS
A LEAP of leopards

LICE
A FLOCK of lice.

LIONS
A PRIDE, FLOCK, SAWT, SOUSE, or TROOP of lions.
A SAULT of lions.

LOCUSTS
A CLOUD, PLAGUE or SWARM of locusts.

LOONS
A RAFT of loons.

MAGPIES

A TITTERING, TIDING, GULP, MURDER or CHARM of
magpies.

MALLARDS

A SORD or BRACE of mallards.

MARES

A STUD of mares.

MARTENS

A RICHNESS of martens.

A RICHESSE of martens.

MEERKATS

A MOB of meerkats.

MICE

A MISCHIEF of mice.
A HORDE of mice.
A HARVEST of mice.
A COLONY of mice.
A NEST of mice.

MINNOWS

A STEAM of minnows.

MOLES

A LABOUR of moles.

MONGOOSES

A BUSINESS of mongooses.

MONKEYS

A TROOP, CARTLOAD or BARREL of monkeys

MOOSE

A HERD of moose.

MOSQUITOES

A SCOURGE of mosquitoes.

MULES
A <u>BARREN</u>, <u>PACK</u> or <u>SPAN</u> of mules.

NIGHTINGALES
A <u>WATCH</u> of nightingales.
An <u>ENCHANTMENT</u> of nightingales.

OTTERS
A <u>FAMILY</u>, <u>BEVY</u> or <u>ROMP</u>* of otters.
A <u>RAFT</u> of otters

OWLS
A <u>PARLIAMENT</u> of owls.
A <u>STARE</u> or <u>WISDOM</u> of owls.
A <u>STUDY</u> of owls.

OXEN
A <u>TEAM</u> or <u>YOKE</u> of oxen..
A <u>DROVE</u> or <u>HERD</u> of oxen
A <u>SPAN</u> of oxen

OYSTERS
A <u>BED</u> of oysters

PARROTS
A <u>PANDEMONIUM</u> or <u>COMPANY</u> of parrots.

PARTRIDGES
A <u>COVEY</u> of partridges

PEACOCKS
A <u>MUSTER</u> or <u>OSTENTATION</u> of peacock.
A <u>PULCHRITUDE</u> of peacocks.

PEEPS
A <u>LITTER</u> of peeps.

PELICANS
A <u>SQUADRON</u> of pelicans.
A <u>POD</u> or <u>SCOOP</u> of pelicans.

PENGUINS
A ROOKERY or COLONY of penguins

PHEASANTS
A HEAD, NYE, NEST, NIDE (BROOD)* or BEVY of pheasants.
A BOUQUET of pheasants (in flight)

PIGEONS
A KIT of pigeons (flying together)
A FLOCK or FLIGHT of pigeons.

PIGS
A HERD, TRIP, or LITTER of pigs
A DRIFT, DROVE, SOUNDER (swine), TEAM, PASSEL (hogs)*

PLOVERS
A STAND, WING, OR CONGREGATION of plovers

PONIES
A DROVE OR STRING of ponies.

PORCUPINES
A PRICKLE of porcupines.

PORPOISES
A HERD, SCHOOL or POD of porpoises.

PRAIRIE DOGS
A COTERIE of prairie dogs.

PTARMIGAN
A COVEY of Ptarmigan

PUGS (breed of dog)
A GRUMBLE of Pugs

PUPS
A LITTER of pups
A PUDDLE of puppies

QUAIL
A BEVY, DRIFT or COVEY of quail

RABBITS
A BURY, COLONY, CIRCLE, NEST, HERD (domestic), LITTER
(young) of rabbits.
A TRACE of rabbits.
A WARREN of rabbits.

RACCOONS
A GAZE of raccoons.Chris Lam
A NURSERY of raccoons.

RACEHORSES
A STRING of racehorses

RATS
A COLONY of rats.
A PACK or SWARM of rats.
A MISCHIEF of rats.

RATTLESNAKES
A RHUMBA of
rattlesnakes.

RAVENS
An UNKINDNESS of ravens.
A MURDER of
ravens.
A CONSPIRACY of
ravens.

REINDEER
A HERD of reindeer.

RHINOS
A CRASH or HERD of rhinos

ROEBUCKS
A BEVY of roebucks.

ROOKS
A BUILDING or ROOKERY of rooks.
A CLAMOUR of rooks.
A PARLIAMENT of rooks

ROTIFERS
(a type of plankton found in lakes and rivers)
A POD of rotifers.

RUFFS
A HILL of ruffs

SARDINES
A FAMILY of sardines.

SASQUATCH
A PUNGENT of sasquatch.

SCHNAUZERS
A STENCH of Schnauzers

SEA OTTERS
A RAFT of sea otters

SEAGULLS
A FLOCK of seagulls.

SEAHORSES
A HERD of seahorses.

SEALS
A HERD, HAREM, TRIP or ROOKERY of seals
A POD of seals (a small herd)

SHARKS
A SHIVER of sharks.

SHEEP
A FLOCK, HERD, HIRSEL, PACK, DROVE or TRIP of sheep
A MOB of sheep (Australian)

SKUNKS
A SURFEIT of skunks.

SKYLARKS
An ASCENSION of skylarks.

SNAKES
A DEN, BED, PIT **or** SLITHER of snakes.
A NEST or KNOT of snakes.
A BROOD of snakes (a family group)

SNIPE
A WISP or WALK of snipe

SPARROWS
A HOST of sparrows.
A KNOT of sparrows.

SQUIRRELS
A DRAY or SCURRY of squirrels.

STARLINGS
A MURMATION of starlings.
A MURMURATION of starlings.
A FILTH of starlings
A CHATTERING of starlings.
An AFFLICTION of starlings.

STINGRAYS
A FEVER of stingrays.

STORKS
A MUSTERING of storks.

SWALLOWS
A FLIGHT or GULP of swallows

SWANS
A GAME, BANK, TEAM, HERD or BEVY of swans.
A WEDGE of swans in the air.
A LAMENTATION of swans.
A BALLET of swans.

SWIFTS
A FLOCK of swifts

SWINE
A HERD, DRIFT OR SOUNDER of swine

TADPOLES
A CLOUD of tadpoles.

TEAL
A SPRING of teal.

TERMITES
A BROOD, COLONY, NEST OR SWARM of termites.

THRUSHES
A MUTATION of thrushes.

TIGERS
An AMBUSH or STREAK of tigers.

TOADS
A KNOT or KNAB of toads

TORTOISES
A CREEP of tortoises.

TROUT
A HOVER of trout.

TURKEYS
A RAFTER or GANG of turkeys.
A CLUTCH of turkeys.

TURTLE DOVES
A PITYING or DULE of turtle doves.

TURTLES
A BALE, DOLE or NEST of turtles.
A TURN of turtles.

UNICORNS
A FANTASY of unicorns.
A BLESSING of unicorns.
A GLORY of unicorns.
A SURPRISE of unicorns.

VIPERS
A NEST of vipers.
A BROOD of vipers.

VULTURES
A COMMITTEE of
vultures.

WALRUSES
A HERD or POD of walruses.

WASPS
A PLADGE of wasps.
A PAIL of wasps.
A NEST of wasps.

WATERFOWL
A BUNCH, KNOB, TRIP or PLUMP of waterfowl

WEASELS
A BOOGLE, GANG, CONFUSION or PACK of weasels.

WHALES
A SCHOOL, HERD or GAM of whales
A POD of whales (small school)
A GRIND of bottle nose whales

WIDGEON
A COMPANY or TRIP of widgeon

WILDFOWL
A BUNCH, TRIP or PLUMP of wildfowl.
A KNOB of wildfowl (less than 30)

WOLVES
A PACK or ROUT of wolves

WOMBATS
A WISDOM of wombats.

WOODCOCKS
A FALL of woodcocks.

WOODPECKERS
A DESCENT of woodpeckers.

WORMS
A CLEW of worms.

WRENS
A HERD of wrens
A CHIME of wrens

ZEBRAS
A ZEAL, HERD or DAZZLE of zebras

$$=== \text{AUTHOR'S NOTES} ===$$

When my niece, Rachel, was just three years old, she had already revealed herself to be quite attentive to, taken by, and enamored with animals of all kinds. Not only could she recognize and name different sounds of birds, but at the local zoo, she knew all of the names of the animals simply by recognizing their shapes and outlines on the zoo's animal location markers — which contained no pictures or identifying details of the animals, per se, but simply depicted them as black silhouettes directing people to the exhibits.

And when I say she knew their names, I'm not talking about the simple, pedestrian, everyday, run-of-the-mill, three-year-old-understood names like "bear" or "cat" — the stuff of mere mortals. She had already memorized the much more scientific, complex, adult-ish name of each of the species we would visit, and like old friends, was able to address them by their full and proper titles — i.e., the "tapir", the "aardvark", the "civet", the "ocelot", the "lemur", the "beluga whale", the "colobus monkey", the ringtail possum', the "black-rumped agouti", and the "naked mole rat", to name just a few.

In fact, I'm pretty sure that if we had gone there just a few more times, she would have been well on her way to learning the Latin names for their genus' and species. I could imagine her now in kindergarten during show-and-tell, telling the kids about her day spent communing with her close friend, the *'canis lupus'* (wolf), or the wild and fierce *'ursus maritimus'* (polar bear) — her favorite bear in the exhibit. That would have been worth a video or two….

At home, she had a collection of plastic animal figurines which we would take out and play with, and I would always ask her to remind me which kinds of animals were which. Now, while most kids at the age of three who saw a collection of large four-legged 'cow' or 'horse'-like creature might defer to calling them all by one general kind of form-fitting name (like 'doggie' or 'horsie'), but even by age two, Rachel could already distinguish between cows, horses, mules, moose, deer, antelope, water buffalo, bison, gnu's, and various other similar looking sorts. Pretty impressive….

To augment her vocabulary, I started to ask her about the names for the young of each of her favorite animals (puppies, kittens, goslings, bittens, etc), and eventually we started delving into the group names you might call each species when they were gathered together (a 'flock' of seagulls, a 'herd' of antelope, a 'parliament' of owls, etc). I would often look these up at the library or online using Wikipedia, and it was a great learning experience for me as well. To make it more fun, I started to invent and eventually jot down some silly little rhyming verses that we could use as mnemonics — a fun way to remember the group names — and that is what ultimately became the inspiration for this book.

If you happen to find it a little whimsical or silly yourself, that's because it's supposed to be! — it was written for a very smart little three year old, with the intention that it could also be something she would be able to grow into down the line, especially given the fact that a few of the vocabulary words used here are something slightly beyond the average three year old's ken of knowledge.

And true to form, that's exactly what happened. In fact, I noticed that several years later, by the age of six or seven, Rachel already seemed familiar with words like "phylogeny", "insomniac", "terrestrial", and "menagerie" — not that she was using them in her regular daily vernacular, but she certainly knew what they meant when asked. (Now I'm not saying it's directly because of this book, but I'm not saying 'not' either. What we do know is that most of the vocabulary and speech patterns that toddlers learn is from direct exposure to what they hear around them when they are young, take that as you will....)

As an aside, I should mention that each of these little stanzas was originally created with the intention of saying them or reading them aloud (something I enjoyed doing with Rachel when she was young). And in this respect, the cadence and rhythm of the verses become a little more important. To help you navigate through some of the rhyme schemes, in a number of the verses where I felt the intended inflections might be a little confusing, I've placed a small line beneath those syllable that contain the beat, pulse, or cadence of the reading. For example, if I were to write:

> *Though s<u>ea</u>gull bird-bl<u>o</u>kes r<u>a</u>rely get j<u>o</u>kes*
> *and their l<u>au</u>gh is the s<u>i</u>lliest I've h<u>ea</u>rd,*
> *comp<u>a</u>red to their p<u>a</u>ls, the l<u>o</u>vely sea g<u>a</u>ls,*
> *I've not s<u>ee</u>n a more g<u>u</u>llible b<u>ir</u>d...*

you will notice that the words "seagull", "blokes", "rarely", and "jokes", etc, have lines placed under those syllable in them that are naturally emphasized in your reading of the piece. I have not done this for all of the verses (I thought that might be a little visually distracting), just for those few lines where I felt there might be some need to clarify.

I hope this helps you with both your reading of the text and with your enjoyment of the pieces.

Enjoy!

=== ABOUT THE AUTHOR ===

Ari Levitt, MD

Physician & Health Advocate;
Faculty Member, Singularity
University's Medical Wing;
Founder & Director, "Roll Up The
Rug & Dance" & "Terpsicorp"

Poet, author, dancer, doctor,
       musician from Bossa to blues,
philosopher, philatelist, creator & catalyst,
       purveyor of unique points of views…

Brother & son, grandson & uncle,
       scientist, explorer, & sage;
A rare and curated gemstone carbuncle,
       frequent guest of the lectern and stage…

Now here to share with *qu'est-ce que c'est, savoir faire,*
       a few humble lines in a style
not meant as profound, nor to change you around,
       but just hoping they bring you a smile!

Ari Levitt, MD

A physician, artist, musician, writer, traveler, teacher, and entrepreneur, Ari completed his undergraduate education in Human Biology & Philosophy at Stanford University; his medical degree at the University of Washington; and his residency in Family Practice in Harrisburg, PA. He currently resides in Seattle, WA, where he actively lectures and teaches.

As a physician, Ari is a leading pioneer in the field of "Experiential Wellness", which combines the best of allopathic medicine with the creative Arts, helping individuals to utilize their hobbies & interests (or 'experiences') to motivate healthy behaviors and to create a richer, more rewarding, and personalized model for wellness in their lives.

Through his company, Terpsicorp, he also brings his rich knowledge of business acumen to corporate settings with unique, interactive, and hands-on presentations that focus on improving productivity and teaching successful leadership and communication skills in the work setting.

Ari is also a renown and much sought after world-class social dance instructor, actively teaching throughout the USA and abroad. With a breadth of styling extending from swing, blues, ballroom, Latin, fusion and beyond, he runs a wide variety of travel and dance adventure programs, including: "Waltz Week in Vienna", "Mexico Dance Adventure", "Waltzfest NW", "Harrison Hot Spring Dance & Spa Retreat", Hawaii Dance Week", "New Zealand Dance Adventure", and "Dancing with Horses", among others, and has been a featured DJ and instructor in various festivals throughout the USA and beyond. You can learn more about Ari at www.rolluptherug.com

<u>**Books from Ari now available on Amazon**</u>

"A Little Dog's Tale"
Stories from a Grateful Pooch

"The Midlife Crisis of Paul Revere"
A New Poetic Take on a Classic Poetic Tale

"Pieces of my Past"
An Eclectic Collection of Original Poetry
(and the events that inspired their writings)

"The Coffee Addict"
A delicious 'roast' of coffee,
well worth the 'poring' over…

"The Ballad of a Tree-Peeing Pooch"
(aka, "The Rhyme of the Ancient Urinator")
Answering the age old question in rhyme, humor, and wit:
"Why do dogs pee on trees?"

"Lovely as You"
A Poem about Love, Appreciation,
and a Little Something Amore

"Animal Communities Revisited"
A Fun & Fabulous Way
to Learn Animal Group Names

"My Passage (Almost) To India"
The Exciting Adventures of a Man, in Limbo,
Nearly Obtaining a Tourist Visa

<u>More Books in the Works</u>

"The Secret Language of Poetry"
A guide to understanding the language of poetry,
and a simple method for getting you started in the craft

"A Danceable Feast"
A very special cookbook
for dancer's, diner's, and music lover's alike…

"A Necessary Indulgence"
How music, dance, & the Arts can save medicine
and bring wellness, balance, & joy to your life!

== **INDEX** ==

ANIMALS REFERENCED IN THIS BOOK

(in alphabetical order)

Snakes	42
Squirrel	40
Stallion	39
Stingrays	15
Swans	19, 34
Tadpoles	40
Termites	35
Tigers	24
Tortoise	14
Trout	18
Turkeys	24
Turtles	38
Turtle Dove	17
Vultures	16
Whales	14
Wolves	23
Wombats	15
Woodpeckers	14, 29
Zebra	21